BRADFORD RINGWALKS

Foreword by Lady Kirk

Member, Countryside Commission.

It is a particular pleasure to me to introduce the Bradford Ringwalks. I lived for twelve years on Manningham Lane, and in those days teenagers could easily get by bus out into one dale, walk over the moors and again find bus or train to get home. For shorter walks the Aire and the canal were natural targets: the first Ringwalk is even better nowadays than I remember it, for the Salt Works and Chapel were grimy black, with no recollection of the gleaming stone we see again today.

Sometimes we went to the other side of Bradford, but it never occurred to us to seek out rural walks all round the city. It needed Dr. Sheldon to show us all how much good country there is so close to town.

The walks are worked out in a most flexible way: one can follow the guide for a short hour, go for several miles or all day. The main round-the-city route is well served by public transport and is shadowed by a second ring of return routes, so that each section can itself be a round walk. Arthur Gemmell's maps are beautifully clear and have the great advantage of being drawn solely for walking. They are not cluttered with irrelevant information, but contain everything one needs to find the way in either direction. That leaves Dr. Sheldon free to write an interesting commentary on things to be seen along the route.

The Countryside Commission is closely involved in work to enhance the country on the city doorstep and to enable people to enjoy it. One way of doing this is by countryside management schemes to conserve the landscape, improve public paths and iron out problems. The Commission has helped to finance one such scheme in Tong and Cockersdale (walks 5 and 6). Another way is to grant aid the publication, at a modest price, of guides such as this which help people to enjoy their heritage.

Dr. Sheldon has made a notable contribution to the health and pleasure of city life. I hope that many Bradfordians, young and old, will follow his lead.

Elizabeth Kirk

March 1982

General Introduction

The walks that are described in this booklet have been developing for well over twenty years. I have been interested in maps and walking as long as I can remember. In the days after the last war when petrol was scarce and my father had to be within easy reach of his patients, our walks took place close to Bradford. My father gave me an old Ordnance Survey 1 inch "Leeds-Bradford" map that had long outlived its usefulness. I put it to use by plotting on it all the walks that we had done and was surprised to note that we had almost totally circumnavigated the city at a radius of about five miles. Naturally this was a stimulus to a young boy and before long by dint of walking along a few boring main roads the circuit was completed. The map adorned my bedroom wall for many years.

Then came University and walking was forgotten and the map tidied away until I returned to Bradford after qualifying as a doctor. One evening about four years ago I found the map again and compared it with a modern Leeds-Bradford map. To my surprise I saw that the walk, with a few modifications, was still possible. More important, considering its closeness to the centre of a large modern city, was the fact that it passed for the most part through remarkably pretty countryside. My idea at first, was that the circuit which measures about 31½ miles would be suitable as an off-road route for more ambitious Sponsored Walks. It is surely more agreeable to walk on pleasant footpaths than soul-destroying main roads. But it was greeted with indifference by both the voluntary organisations that I approached.

So I returned to my maps and on closer inspection I found that it would be easy to divide the walk into 14 parts, each with a return route thereby making 14 circular walks ranging from 2½ to 8 miles in length and hence within reach of anyone who is reasonably agile. Car parking is easy at some point on any walk and all the walks at one point or another cross or pass near to bus routes.

As regards that which I will call the main route of 31½ miles, there are no rules about its completion. Walking is meant to be pleasant and you can take as little or as long as you like about completing it. It took my wife about a year. I did it once, all in one go and I do not fancy that I shall repeat the performance. If you do it in bits you will enjoy parts of our city that you may not have seen before at a fraction of the travelling cost of a journey to the more famous walking country in the Dales.

How to Use the Booklet

Read this introduction and page 28. Study the key map and the symbols on page 5. Select the walk of your choice, turn to the appropriate route map and read the text opposite. If you are an accomplished map reader the A to Z Leeds and Bradford street map, the Bradford Metropolitan District Map or the Ordnance Survey

2½" maps are of more use than the 1" in city areas. These preliminaries are well worthwhile to ensure that features of interest on the walk are not missed and to enable a reasonable estimate to be made of the time to allow for the walk.

It is naturally possible to combine some of the shorter walks to make longer ones. The walk also links with the Calderdale Way, the Dalesway and the Leeds Country Way. In all cases the walks are designed to start and finish at a convenient point.

With the exception of two, all the walks are done best by starting on the main route in a generally clockwise direction and coming back on the return route. At first I started the walk in an anti-clockwise direction. I soon realised that the views are generally better when done in the direction I have indicated.

Explanation of the Route Maps

The maps have been specially drawn by Arthur Gemmell for easy interpretation by showing only features and information relative to the walk. I drew the original (very) rough drafts and these have been produced into their present form by Arthur Gemmell to whom I am very grateful for all his help, advice and wisdom. If it were not for him the map would still be on the wall of my bedroom. Likewise the text has been perused and improved by my father and I am grateful to him also.

The walk has been totally walked three times by myself and once by Arthur Gemmell in the last two years. The paths shown are rights of way by long usage. Any difficulties should be reported to the Footpaths Officers at Jacobs Well House, Bradford or at the County Hall, Wakefield (if outside the city boundary).

It would be appreciated if changes to other important features such as field boundaries, stiles and path movements are reported to the publishers for future editions. The maps contain all the information necessary to follow the route correctly.

My thanks are also due to Lady Kirk for the Foreword and to the Countryside Commission, the City of Bradford Metropolitan Council and the West Yorkshire Metropolitan County Council for helpful information and suggestions.

The Character of Bradford

In many ways Bradford is still, even today, a village surrounded by a large number of smaller villages which have merged to give the City we know today. It is situated in a branch from the great valley of the River Aire in West Yorkshire and part of this walk follows the river for some miles. Apart from the valley leading from the centre of Bradford to the Aire, the city is constructed in a large hollow surrounded by hills on three sides which range in height from 600 to over 1200 feet. The walk tends to follow these hills and explains the superb views that are such a surprising feature. As well as the river, part of the walk also follows the Leeds-Liverpool canal, but by far the largest proportion is on paths through woods or fields. The fences or walls surrounding the fields are usually penetrated by narrow stiles and so regrettably are not suitable for the physically handicapped. However, the stretches on the canal are smooth and level and even wheel-chairs could be pushed along the towpath, which is only narrowed in the section to the west of Field Locks in Esholt.

I am particularly proud of the fact that, as regards the main route, only about a mile is on motor roads and less than a quarter of a mile on my pet horror—main roads. Wherever the walk crosses a main road or goes through a village it amost goes without saying that shops, pubs, telephones and chippies will be there in profusion. However, telephones are not to be relied on, usually being out of order. I was once very grateful to the Greengrocer in Birkenshaw for allowing me to use her telephone when I was marooned ten miles away from my wife!

In many ways the walk reflects the character of modern Britain. Children might find it interesting to make a note of the number of sports they see being played in various places on the walk. I remember particularly a furious game of cricket being played at Thornbury between a Pakistani and a West Indian team with supporters whose cheering would rival any kop.

General Notes on the Walks

All the walks are easy and there is no stiff climbing or scrambling. But sometimes many of the walks are very muddy and stout boots will be required in winter and spring. Even so there is a lot to be said for winter walking and I remember a delightful snowy morning when we started walking at about 8 o'clock in Thornton. We began on the return route of Walk 12 and looking across towards Clayton from Leavensthorpe School we saw the children coming to school across the snow covered meadow and the whole scene was reminiscent of Lowry with the little figures scampering over the snow.

The paths are mostly clearly visible and even if they are not, the stiles can be seen for many hundreds of yards. In one or two cases the path goes through what at first looks like a garden. It is but do not be discouraged, walkers seem to be welcomed.

Finally, please enjoy this. I have enjoyed putting it together and realised more than ever how lucky I am to live in such a surprisingly beautiful city.

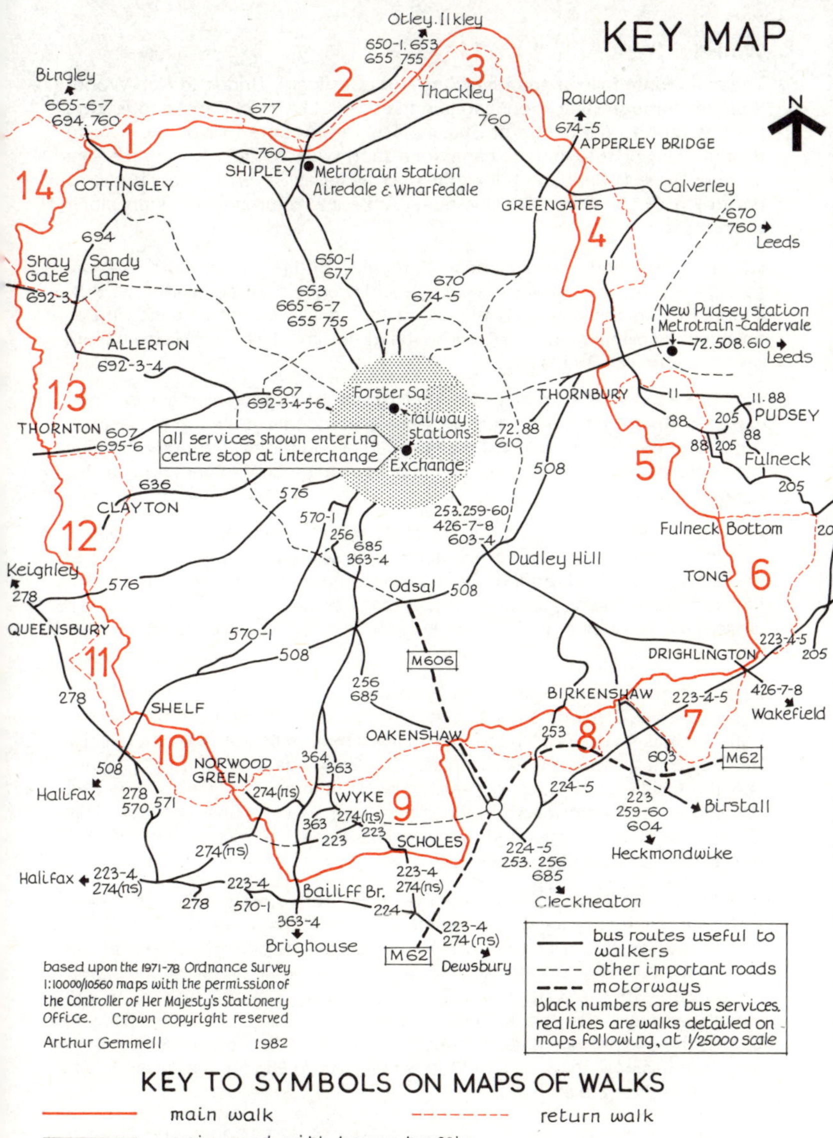

KEY TO SYMBOLS ON MAPS OF WALKS

main walk — return walk

main road with heavy traffic

minor road or lane with little or no traffic

wall, fence or hedge, showing gateway

river and stream (arrow shows direction of flow)

footbridge — △ hill top — trees

S stile — P parking space — steep hillside

Fork left → These notes in red panels appear where walkers could lose the path and apply only if going in the recommended direction (thus →). The way goes clockwise around Bradford for the main route

Walk 1

The main route follows the River Aire from Cottingley Bridge to Nab Wood. It passes through Hirst Woods to join the Leeds-Liverpool Canal and follows the tow-path to the centre of Shipley. The return route follows the river to Saltaire, leaving it to join the canal for a short while before crossing the Aire to enter Roberts Park and follow the river as far as Seven Arches. It rejoins the tow-path as far as the Fishermans Arms and returns to the start along Wagon Lane.

I sometimes wonder why I chose Cottingley Bridge as the start. A more sensible place might be, say the George and Dragon at Apperley Bridge. But, I thought that the final long pull along the canal was not as satisfying as finishing the climbing at Allerton with the route almost all downhill from there on. So Cottingley Bridge it is.

Almost immediately the path passes underneath the huge water mains carrying water for Bradford from Nidderdale to the Waterworks at the top of Haworth Road. The path used to cut off the large U bend in the river but now Bingley RUFC have spread across the river and as usual when something like this happens the notices proliferate.

A superb walled path goes along the bottom of the Bankfield Hotel grounds and this is followed by an attractive riverside stretch albeit with Nab Wood Cemetery in the background. Hirst Wood seems to be common land with paths going in every direction but our path comes out to Hirst Lock and crosses the swing bridge. Sadly the little farm-house that sold ice-cream is no longer there.

If refreshments are required it means continuing along the tow-path past Salts Football Ground, Salts Cricket Ground and, across in Roberts Park, Saltaire Cricket Ground. On the right is the famous village of Saltaire built by Sit Titus Salt to house his mill-workers. The Congregational Church is superb and the inside quite startling. As Shipley is entered the new Income Tax building is on the left and 'Water Prince' may be seen on the water. This floating restaurant is operated by the Apollo Canal Co. and serves delicious meals using entirely fresh foods.

The return path beside the river is surfaced but rather narrow. This is in contrast to the path in Roberts Park which was presented to the City in 1920 by Sir James Roberts. It had originally been set out as part of Saltaire by Sir Titus Salt. Well beyond the far end the odd looking stone igloos are something to do with the waterworks. The next stretch of river is quite wide and straight and is the headquarters of the Bradford Grammar School Rowing Club who have produced many famous rowers such as Boris Rankin in their time. But it is wise to beware of furious coaches cycling fanatically along the rough path shouting at their crews.

Seven Arches is a splendid and rare example of a canal aqueduct. The masonry is appropriately massive to carry the weight of the canal and a path on either side. The locks that follow (Dowley Gap) are an excellent example of a type of lock rarely found elsewhere in Britain. In the staircase lock, the top gate of one lock forms the bottom gate of the lock above enabling the canal to gain height quickly. Here the staircase is only of two rises—the famous one at Bingley has five. The final stretch is past Wagon Lane Tip but it will probably end up like the sportsfield at Hirst Woods. For that was one too.

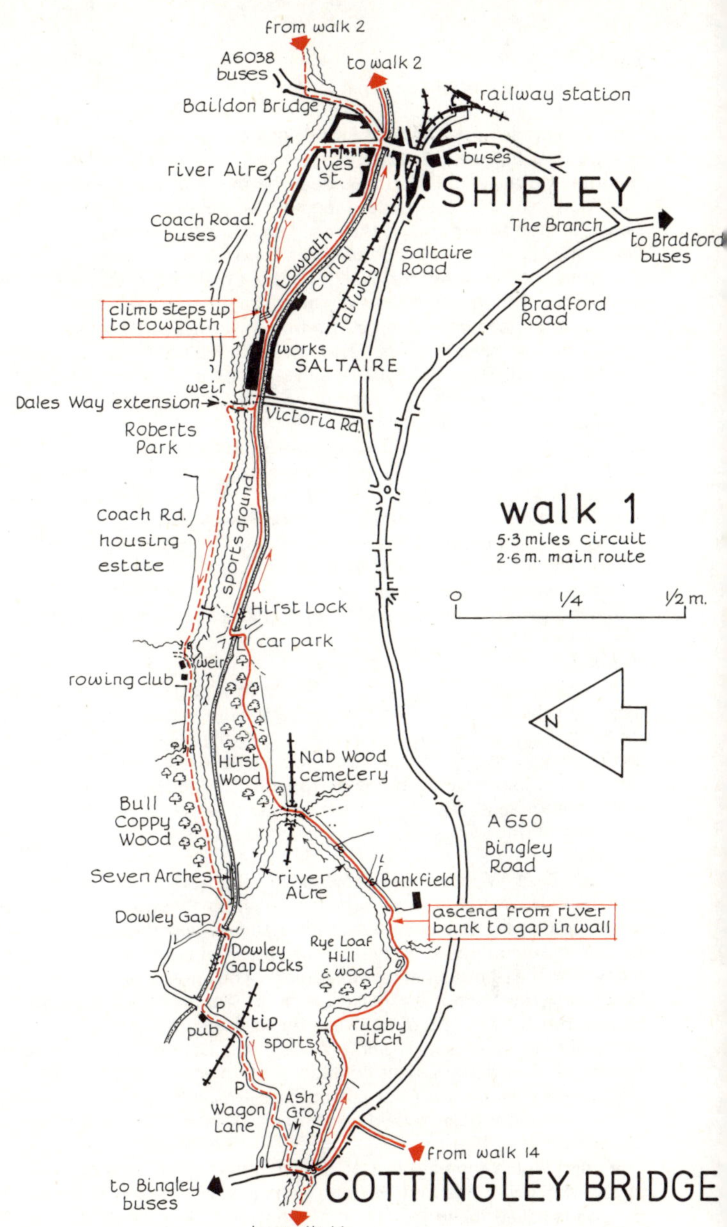
from walk 2
A6038
buses
to walk 2
railway station
Baildon Bridge
river Aire
Ives
St.
buses
SHIPLEY
Coach Road
buses
The Branch
to Bradford
buses
towpath
canal
railway
Saltaire
Road
Bradford
Road
climb steps up
to towpath
works
SALTAIRE
weir
Dales Way extension
Victoria Rd.
Roberts
Park
Coach Rd.
housing
estate
sports ground
walk 1
5·3 miles circuit
2·6 m. main route
0
1/4
1/2 m.
Hirst Lock
car park
weir
rowing club
N
Hirst
Wood
Nab Wood
cemetery
Bull
Coppy
Wood
A 650
Bingley
Road
Seven Arches
river
Aire
Bankfield
Dowley Gap
ascend from river
bank to gap in wall
Dowley
Gap Locks
Rye Loaf
Hill
& wood
P
tip
pub
sports
rugby
pitch
P
Wagon
Lane
Ash
Gro.
from walk 14
to Bingley
buses
COTTINGLEY BRIDGE
to walk 14

Walk 2

The main route follows the canal to Buck Woods Swing Bridge then crosses the river to return to Shipley along the riverside on a most interesting path.

The walk starts at the back of Ellis Briggs cycle shop. Ellis Briggs still make fine bicycles but the memories go back to the early fifties when Ken Russell mounted on the sole Ellis-Briggs beat the might of the works teams to win the Tour of Britain. Palmy days indeed! Shortly the walk passes under the beautiful little roving bridge that used to carry the tow-path over the main line of the canal to the now defunct Bradford Canal.

The canal soon enters more rural ground but first on the left passes the Metal Box works. I long pondered the name, for metal boxes seem thin on the ground to engage such a large firm until I learnt that they manufacture the machines that make tin cans. The railway on the right is the line from Leeds to Glasgow and from Shipley one can take one of the finest day trips on any railway over the metals of the famous Settle-Carlisle line. It is tragic that this line is at present in grave danger of closure.

Just before Buck Woods the main route is left as the river is crossed on a fine cast iron bridge. The path is one of the least known but fascinating paths in Bradford. There is a notice to say that the riverside walk is unsafe for pedestrians but it is all right for the agile. However, it is wise to keep as near to the river as possible and cautious walkers should wear a life jacket and safety helmet! There are several interesting tips where exotic weeds may be found as well as many antique bottles. The path is indicated at the far end by a sign in a garage forecourt and for part of its length is paved. Remarkable!

Walk 3

The path starts at Buck Woods Swing Bridge but it is not possible to approach this by car. It is better to park either on Ainsbury Avenue or at Apperley Bridge. The route continues along the canal tow-path to the main line railway bridge where it leaves the canal and follows a path through the fields to the George and Dragon at Apperley Bridge. The return route is again along the tow-path leaving it at the railway bridge to climb through Dawson Woods and Buck Woods before returning to the swing bridge at the start of the walk.

Through Buck Woods it is worthwhile looking out for that most beautiful of British birds—the Kingfisher which flits along the water. Field Locks are similar to Dowley Gap except that the staircase, like those of Dobson Locks further on, is composed of three locks instead of two. Esholt Sewage Works follow and are of more interest than most. The huge pipes that pass over the canal carry sewage but are unlikely to burst. There is a popular myth that the Works run at a profit by selling chemicals extracted from wool waste. But sadly this is not true—a surplus was only made once and that back in the forties! Until recently Esholt boasted of its own railway and the lines and bridges can still be seen but the engines, of which the most famous was Nellie have now been retired. Nellie can be seen in Bradford's Industrial Museum.

The point where the path passes underneath the railway is the lowest point of the whole walk at about 190 feet. Perhaps a celebration at the George and Dragon is called for to look for the tree that once grew up through the bar and out of the roof! The return route is notable for the excellent views while climbing alongside the railway as it prepares to enter Thackley Tunnel and again in the woods when a panorama of the whole works can be seen. The time to walk here is spring for the bluebells are so colourful.

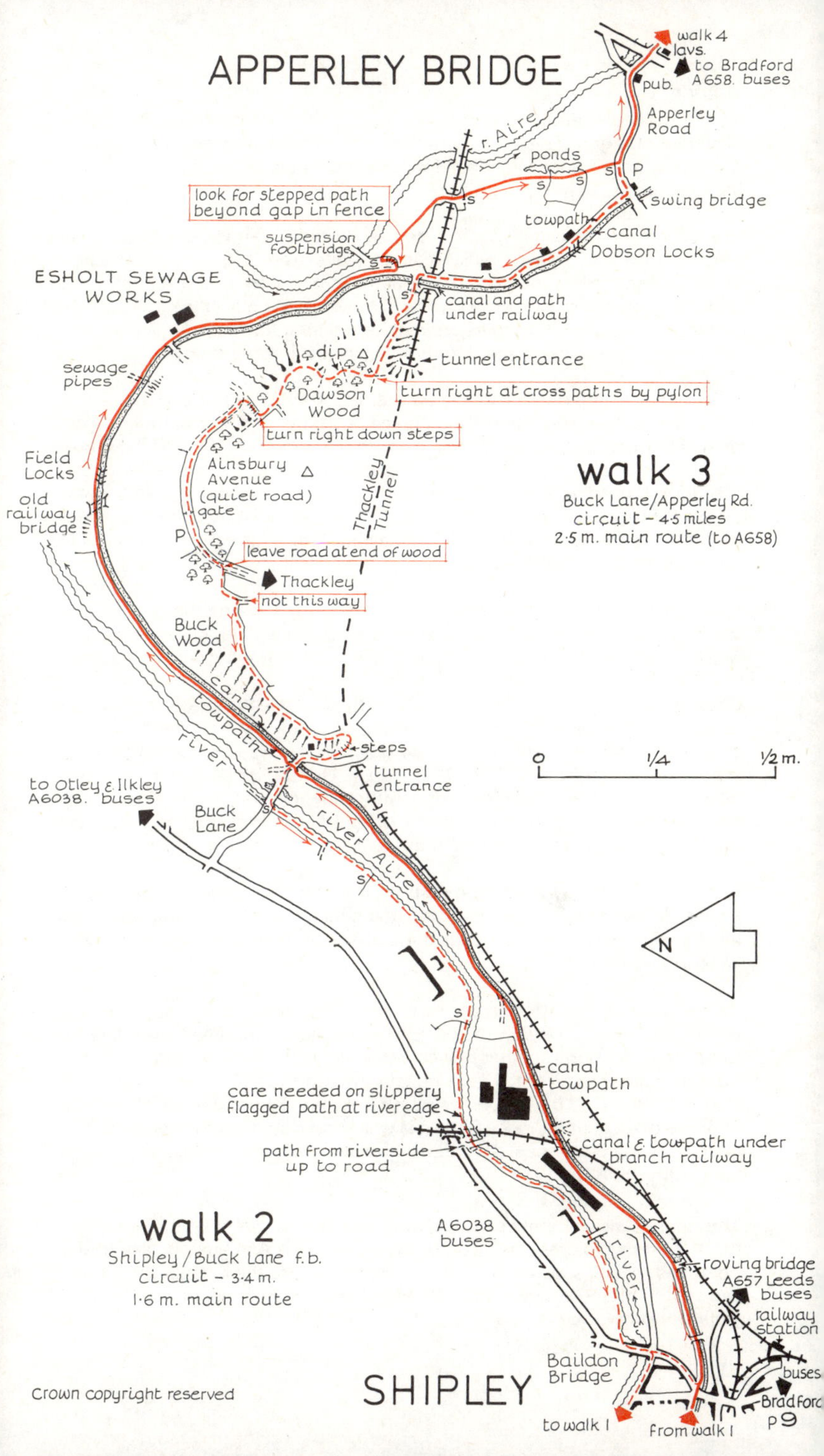
APPERLEY BRIDGE
walk 4
lavs.
to Bradford
A658. buses
pub.
Apperley
Road
r. Aire
ponds
P
swing bridge
look for stepped path
beyond gap in fence
towpath
canal
Dobson Locks
suspension
footbridge
ESHOLT SEWAGE
WORKS
canal and path
under railway
dip
tunnel entrance
sewage
pipes
Dawson
Wood
turn right at cross paths by pylon
turn right down steps
Field
Locks
Ainsbury
Avenue
(quiet road)
walk 3
Buck Lane/Apperley Rd.
circuit – 4·5 miles
2·5 m. main route (to A658)
old
railway
bridge
gate
Thackley
Tunnel
P
leave road at end of wood
Thackley
not this way
Buck
Wood
canal
towpath
river
steps
tunnel
entrance
0
1/4
1/2 m.
to Otley & Ilkley
A6038. buses
Buck
Lane
river
Aire
N
canal
towpath
care needed on slippery
flagged path at river edge
canal & towpath under
branch railway
path from riverside
up to road
A6038
buses
walk 2
Shipley/Buck Lane f.b.
circuit – 3·4 m.
1·6 m. main route
river
roving bridge
A657 Leeds
buses
railway
station
buses
Baildon
Bridge
SHIPLEY
Bradford
P9
to walk 1
from walk 1

Walk 4

At last the main route leaves the Aire Valley, climbing up Fagley Beck and, circling a quarry, crosses a new golf course and fields to reach Thornbury. The return route is viá Woodhall Hills, the new golf course again, Calverley and the famous Calverley Cutting.

The path over the canal which becomes Calverley Cutting is probably the remains of an old railway which carried stone from a quarry to the canal while Eleanor Drive and other wide paths in the vicinity are probably the remains of an abortive building project in Calverley Woods in the last century. A number of Nissen Huts were erected here during the last war. These were later used as a fireworks factory until a fatal explosion occurred.

After crossing the main road the path enters Round Wood and across the beck can be seen the eponymous housing estate. But the path is still remarkably rural. In some ways this is the most important path of the whole circuit for it marks the minute strip of green which still separates Leeds and Bradford. If building were to take place in this wood the cities would become one. As it is one can still walk in solitude in the knowledge that over the hill to the left is the Carr Hill Estate while Ravenscliffe is far enough away not to be intrusive except for the occasional ice-cream van chimes.

It is important to find the left turn from the path towards the quarry. If in doubt make for the tall stone crusher! If it is missed and it is still opening time one could be delayed for hours in the Blue Pig Inn as it sells some fine beers.

Circling round the top of the quarry the path emerges on to a brand new golf course. One compensation for the felling of some trees is that as well as extensive views over Leeds there are now also views right beyond the far side of the walk of Soil Hill and Ilkley Moor. On the right is the disused railway line which used to run from Shipley through Idle and Eccleshill to Dudley Hill Junction. Just before the main road are the cricket pitches where the match I mentioned in the preface took place.

The return is equally rural. The path leaves Woodhall Lane just beyond an ancient horse trough and crosses the golf course again. It sometimes strikes me that golf is rather like doing the same walk over and over again. But *chacun a son gout.*

As the walk returns to Calverley the views are of the north and Rawdon Billing comes into view with much of Airedale. The planes from Leeds/Bradford Airport make themselves heard as well as seen and Horsforth Church is also prominent. The contrast between the mid-fifties semis of the Carr Hill Estate and the properties round Salisbury Street is quite instructive. The final descent of Calverley Cutting is well known but nonetheless interesting in the contrast between the industrial scenes of years gone by and the tranquillity today.

The connecting link between this walk and the next is a little longer than usual for it has to cross the main Bradford to Leeds A647 road which at this point has several shops and a Cavalier Steak Bar for the ravenously hungry. The route continues down Daleside Road past one of the smallest cricket grounds I know, that of Thornbury CC.

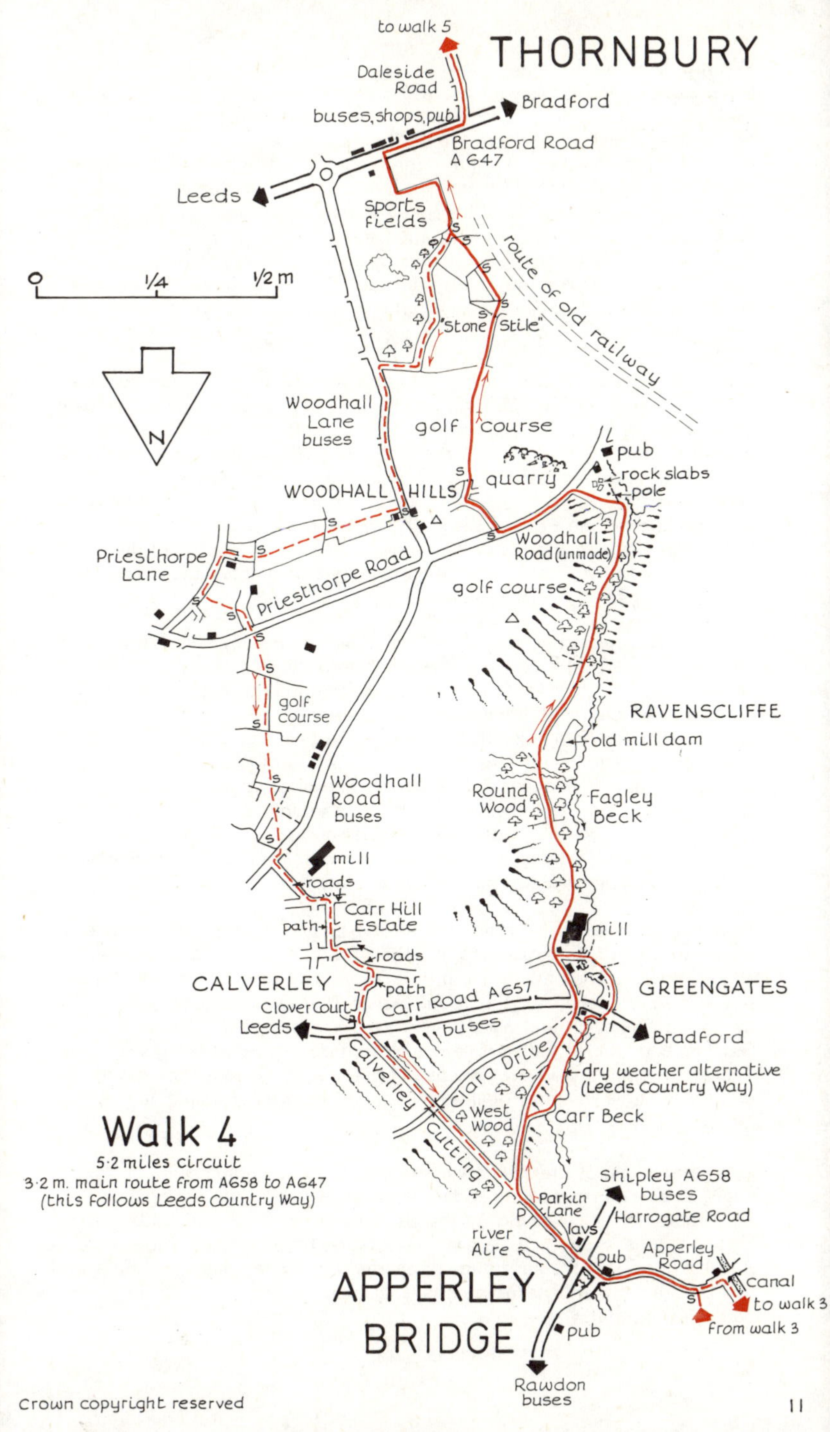
to walk 5
THORNBURY
Daleside Road
Bradford
buses, shops, pub
Bradford Road A 647
Leeds
Sports fields
route of old railway
0
1/4
1/2 m
"Stone Stile"
N
Woodhall Lane buses
golf course
pub
quarry
rock slabs
pole
WOODHALL HILLS
Woodhall Road (unmade)
Priesthorpe Lane
Priesthorpe Road
golf course
golf course
RAVENSCLIFFE
old mill dam
Woodhall Road buses
Round Wood
Fagley Beck
mill
roads
Carr Hill Estate
path
mill
roads
CALVERLEY
path
GREENGATES
Carr Road A657
Clover Court
Leeds
buses
Bradford
Clara Drive
Calverley Cutting
dry weather alternative (Leeds Country Way)
West Wood
Carr Beck
Walk 4
5·2 miles circuit
3·2 m. main route from A658 to A647
(this follows Leeds Country Way)
Shipley A658 buses
Parkin Lane
Harrogate Road
river Aire
lavs
pub
Apperley Road
canal
to walk 3
from walk 3
APPERLEY BRIDGE
pub
Rawdon buses

Walk 5

From Daleside Road this walk crosses a level crossing and proceeds to the West Royd Hill region of Pudsey by means of bridle tracks. It descends to the Holme Valley from where the return route climbs up through Fulneck over the top of West Royd Hill through the centre of Pudsey and returns to the start via the edge of the Stanningley By-Pass and the Chatsworth Estate(!) It is worthwhile looking round before even starting the walk for the Phoenix Golf Course on the right has an interesting history. It was made for its employees by the paternalistic owners of the factory at Thornbury. Known as the Dick Kerr Works, they made tram cars. They even anticipated women's lib by having a Ladies' Soccer Team who were practically World Champions at the time.

The level crossing is over the main Bradford to Leeds line. If you are lucky the occasional Inter City 125 High Speed Train may be seen on its slow way from Bradford to Leeds. But be careful to listen for the bell warning that a train is coming. Further, where the walk drops down to Tyersal Beck the construction is of old fashioned 'setts' which are unfortunately being ripped up by horses as they struggle for grip on the sharp descent. Tyersal Beck goes on to become Pudsey Beck, then Farnley Beck and finally Wortley Beck before it joins the River Aire under Leeds City Station. On the steep bank nearby many of the local young motor cyclists practice their skills away from the main road. And it looks better fun as well.

As the walk approaches West Royd Hill a disused railway embankment will be seen and later the path crosses the approach to a tunnel. This Great Northern line ran from Dudley Hill junction through Pudsey to Leeds. As the path passes a crag and drops into Holme Valley it is obvious that the valley has already been befriended by walkers. Notices have been defaced by local cowboys using them for target practice but the paths are well cared for. Shortly the path joins Fulneck Golf Course and where the path joins Keeper Lane is the junction of the ways. The main walk continues in Walk 6 to Tong while the return route climbs to Fulneck as another superb panorama unfolds. The famous Moravian community in Fulneck was established in 1744 and the school, in particular, has a high reputation.

From the top of West Royd Hill the view is magnificent considering its modest height of about 630 feet. Leeds and Bradford can be seen and the view is almost circular. The path drops to Pudsey and two disused air vents for the tunnel can be seen. As the route leaves Pudsey it passes Pudsey St. Lawrence cricket ground where such great Yorkshire cricketers as Herbert Sutcliffe and Len Hutton were raised. Hutton also attended Fulneck School. There is also another lovely view as the path enters Queens Park recreation ground and on a clear day Beamsley Beacon can be seen poking up over the moors.

From the far end of Queens Park a return all along the road can be made but I have an aversion to walking on tar macadam and so an interesting diversion on a footpath which overlooks the Stanningley By-Pass and Pudsey New Station is used. From here there is no alternative to the road back to the start. But this does have the advantage of passing through a housing estate. I say this because my wife takes a certain vicarious delight in inspecting other people's property!

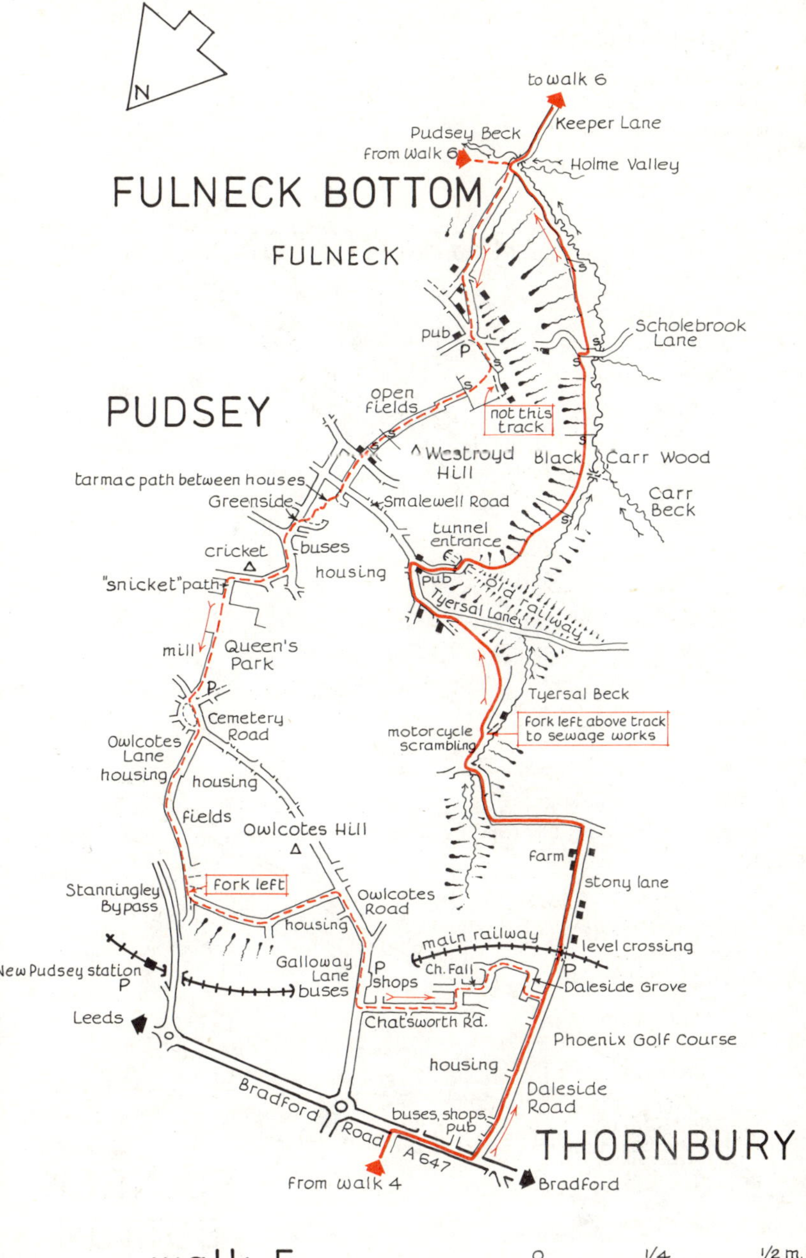

walk 5

5·4 miles circuit

2·7 m. main route from A647. This follows Leeds Country Way

walk 6

4·7 miles circuit
1·8 m. main route (to A650)
The return route follows the Leeds Country Way from the A58

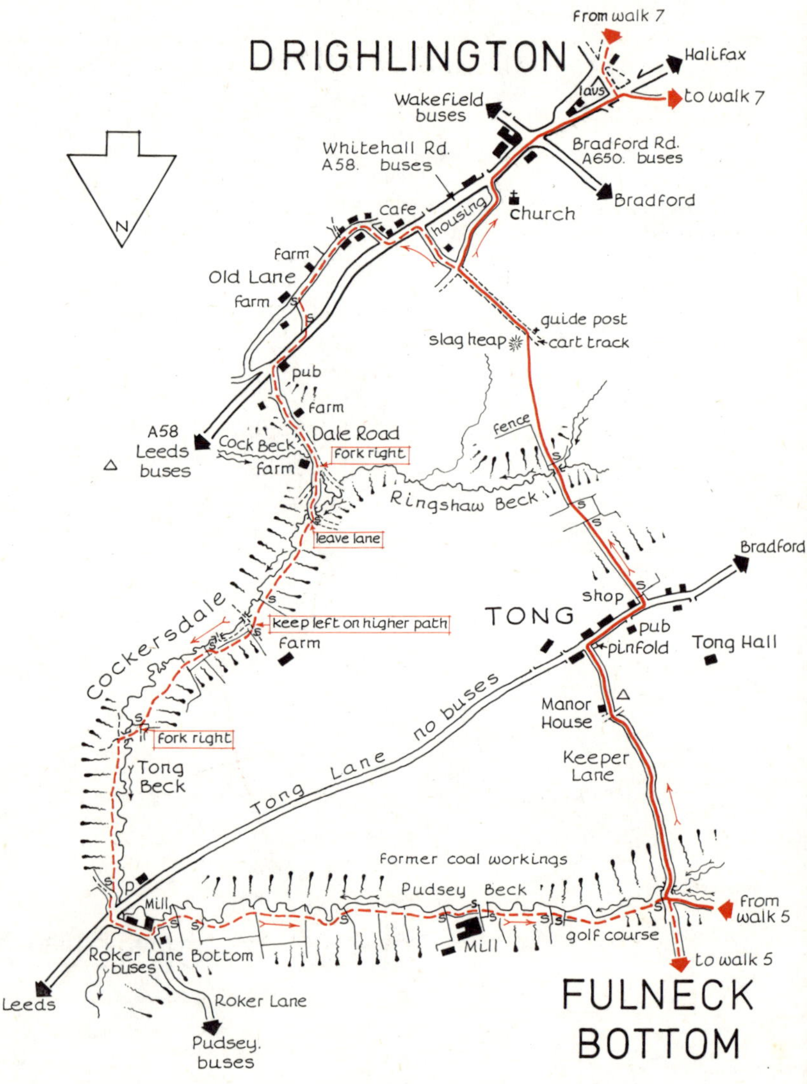

Walk 6

This is one of only two walks that does not start at a convenient parking place so buses must be used or the walk commenced in the middle, say, at Tong. It actually starts from Fulneck bottom, climbs up to Tong and continues to Drighlington Church. The return route is a familiar one to keen walkers as it goes down the popular Cockersdale and returns to the start from Roker Lane Bottom alongside Pudsey Beck.

Keeper Lane in its lower part is still paved. These paths are becoming rarer and ought to be guarded for they are precious. Horses and cows seem to be their worst enemies because their hooves break and tear up the paving stones. The fields on either side of Keeper Lane as it climbs to Tong have undergone as violent a transformation as any part of the walk. When I was young the scene was one of idyllic green fields with a fine view of Fulneck. Then when I was a teenager the fields were torn apart by the open cast mining of fire-clay only to be returned amazingly to the idyllic green fields they now are. From this track can also be seen the fine 18th century Tong Hall—the oldest brick building in the old city of Bradford. Also visible is the old Manor House which is even older.

As the track joins the road on the right look at the old village pump and the beautifully preserved pinfold. This, the notice informs the passer-by was used to keep stray animals in until their owners came to claim them.

From Tong the 19th century St. Pauls Church, Drighlington can be seen with its squat tower and the path makes directly for this, crossing Ringshaw Beck, which joins Pudsey Beck at the bottom of Cockersdale on the way. From Drighlington it is prefectly easy to start the return route along the main Whitehall Road amid the hurly-burly of smoking articulated lorries. But it is far more pleasant to walk along the old road which is much quieter so that thought or conversation can be carried on in peace. The walk returns to the Whitehall Road by some steps and quickly escapes from the traffic into beautiful Cockersdale. It really is quite remarkable that such a pretty little valley can still exist within four miles of the very centre of one of the larger cities in the country. London should be so lucky! It almost seems a shame to mention it in case someone comes along and spoils it. So walk down it in thankfulness.

If anything the return up Pudsey Beck now the opencast mining has ceased is even more remarkable. This is especially so in its early stages. People who know about these things have discovered Cockersdale and it is quite busy in summer with picnickers and the happy sounds of children playing. Pudsey Beck is very quiet indeed but later on a scruffy mill yard spoils the illusion for a while. But soon Fulneck Golf Course is encountered again and the start of the walk is soon reached.

The best places for parking are in Tong Village or at the junction of the Ring-shaw and Pudsey Becks at Roker Lane Bottom.

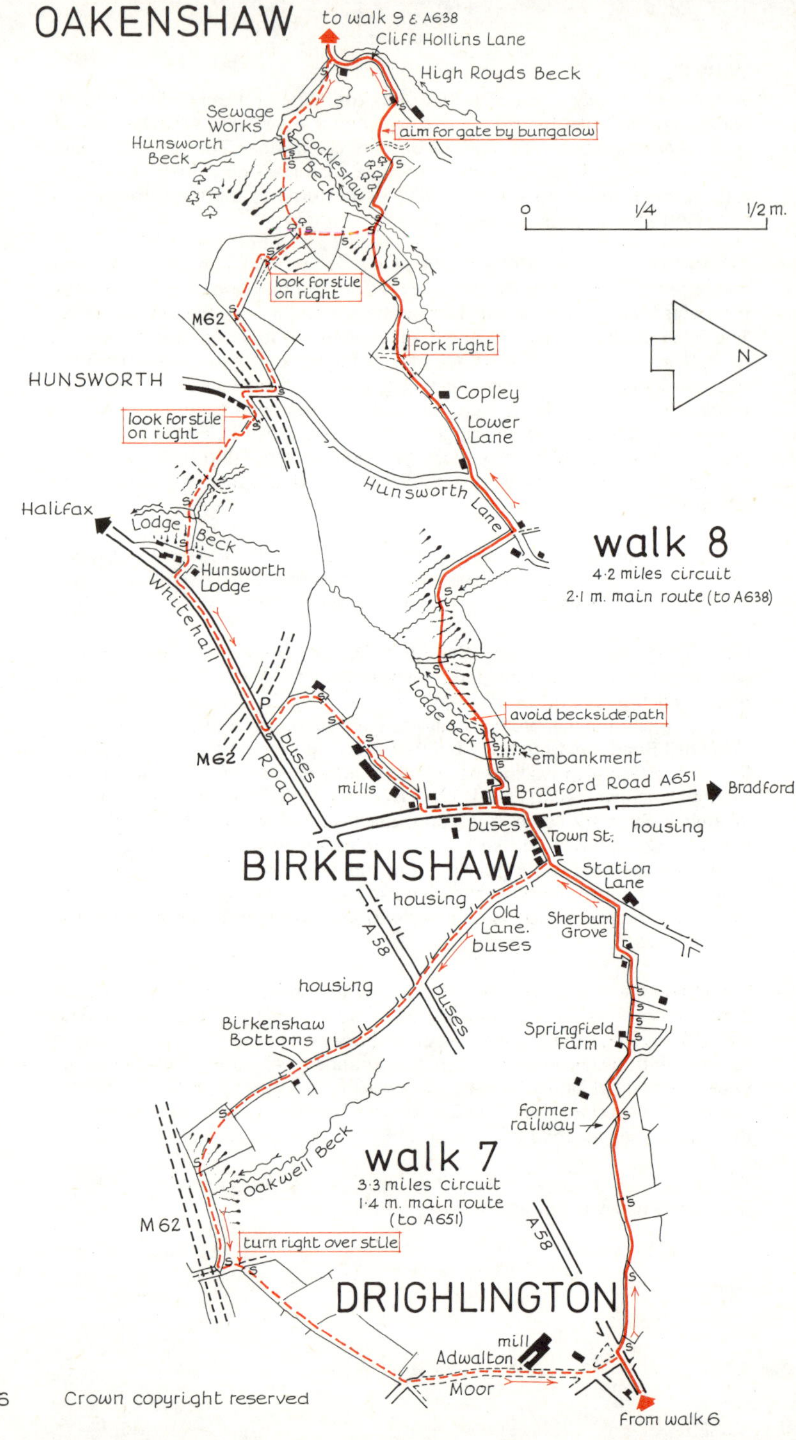
OAKENSHAW
to walk 9 & A638
Cliff Hollins Lane
High Royds Beck
Sewage Works
Hunsworth Beck
Cockleshaw Beck
aim for gate by bungalow
0
1/4
1/2 m.
look for stile on right
M62
fork right
N
HUNSWORTH
Copley
Lower Lane
look for stile on right
Hunsworth Lane
Halifax
Lodge Beck
Hunsworth Lodge
walk 8
4·2 miles circuit
2·1 m. main route (to A638)
Whitehall Road
Lodge Beck
avoid beckside path
embankment
M62
buses
mills
Bradford Road A651
Bradford
buses
Town St.
housing
BIRKENSHAW
Station Lane
housing
Old Lane. buses
Sherburn Grove
A 58
housing
buses
Birkenshaw Bottoms
Springfield Farm
Former railway
Oakwell Beck
walk 7
3·3 miles circuit
1·4 m. main route (to A651)
M 62
A 58
turn right over stile
DRIGHLINGTON
mill
Adwalton
Moor
From walk 6

Walk 7

This section, one of the shortest on the entire route travels from Drighlington to Birkenshaw across the fields. After passing through Birkenshaw village the return route passes along and eventually over the M62. After re-crossing the motorway the way is across perhaps the most historic and famous ground on the whole walk—Adwalton Moor.

The divergence of the path from the Whitehall Road is indicated by a footpath sign. Initially the path goes along the back of an egg factory where the chief interest is all the old and often wrecked lorries. The path crosses a disused railway line which was another Great Northern Line, this time from Dudley Hill to Dewsbury. Springfield Farm is shortly arrived at but contains some wild and ferocious dogs. Luckily these have always (to date) been chained up. Previously the path from here was very decayed but recently some fine and capacious stiles have been erected and the route between two gardens into Sherborn Grove made much more obvious.

On the return route the motorway is crossed twice. Whether this is good or bad depends on personal preference. The view behind as Adwalton is approached is excellent to the south and west.

Adwalton Moor was the scene of one of the great battles in British history. It was fought in 1643 between the Roundheads and Cavaliers. The Roundheads coming from Bradford attacked the Royalists, led by the Earl of Newcastle on the moor. At first they seemed to gain an advantage but an attack by Royalist pikemen won the day and Lord Fairfax's men were chased back to Bradford by the Earl of Newcastle who spent the night in Bolling Hall. The successful general was deterred from sacking Bradford by a benevolent ghost who advised him to "Pity Poor Bradford".

Walk 8

This walk goes from Birkenshaw across the fields to Copley and turns west to Oakenshaw. The return route of this fairly short walk is a little tricky as the path is not very clear. After crossing the M62 the route descends to Lodge Beck and the Whitehall Road is again encountered for a while. The return to Birkenshaw is along a little lane behind the ambulance depot.

As the path leaves Birkenshaw to descend a field an embankment is seen. This is the remains of Emmett's Canal which was built in 1782 by John Emmett to bring coal and ironstone to his furnace. It was closed in 1815. The whole scene here is remarkably rural. Clover, buttercups, wild roses and blackberries abound while the view from Copley is very fine. It extends over 270° and Honley, Emley Moor, Holme Moss and right round to Queensbury are well seen.

Between Copley and Oakenshaw, Cockleshaw Beck is crossed. This becomes Hunsworth Beck then eventually joins Lodge Beck and becomes the Spen River which joins the Calder between Dewsbury and Mirfield and has given its name to the area—Spenborough.

On the return route do not take the track into the sewage works! Instead follow a path, cross the stream by a derelict bridge and make for the clump of trees on the skyline. This enables the walker to find the path which goes to Hunsworth Lane where the route crosses the motorway. Once again Whitehall Road is joined. This is the A58 and one of Britain's older trunk roads. It actually goes from Wetherby to Liverpool, though quite why anyone should want to make that journey is difficult to see. Now the M62 is completed it is considerably more pleasant to travel on than it used to be.

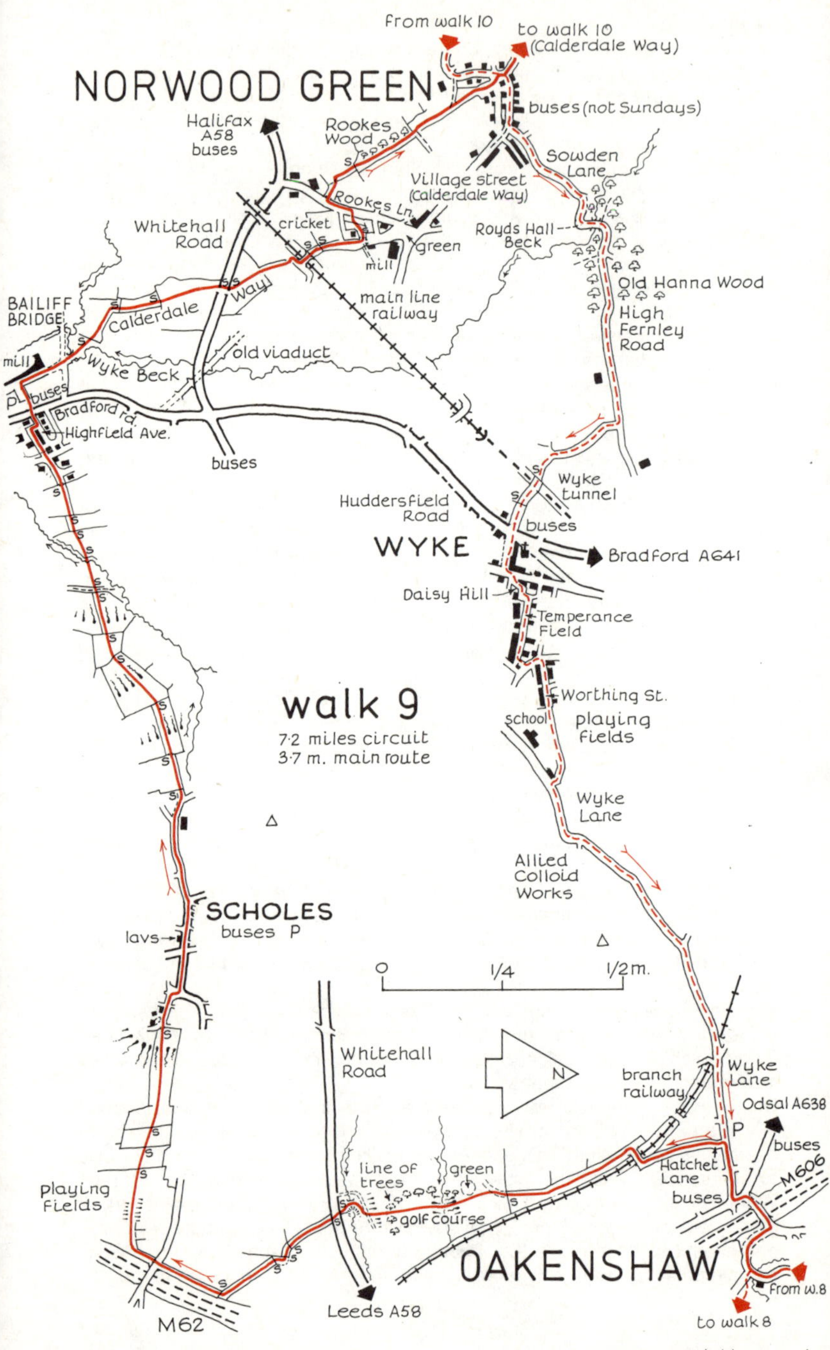
from walk 10
to walk 10 (Calderdale Way)
NORWOOD GREEN
buses (not Sundays)
Halifax A58 buses
Rookes Wood
Sowden Lane
Village street (Calderdale Way)
Rookes Ln.
Whitehall Road
cricket
green
Royds Hall Beck
mill
Old Hanna Wood
High Fernley Road
BAILIFF BRIDGE
Calderdale Way
main line railway
mill
old viaduct
Wyke Beck
P
buses
Bradford rd.
Highfield Ave.
buses
Wyke tunnel
Huddersfield Road
buses
WYKE
Bradford A641
Daisy Hill
Temperance Field
Worthing St.
school
playing fields
walk 9
7·2 miles circuit
3·7 m. main route
Wyke Lane
Allied Colloid Works
SCHOLES
buses P
lavs
0
1/4
1/2 m.
Whitehall Road
N
branch railway
Wyke Lane
Odsal A638
P
buses
line of trees
green
Hatchet Lane
M606
buses
playing fields
golf course
OAKENSHAW
From w.8
to walk 8
Leeds A58
M62

Walk 9

Oakenshaw is just over halfway round if the walk is started from Cottingley. It is about 18 miles and this is celebrated by the fact that this circular walk is the longest of the fourteen. It is also, I think the one that seems least part of Bradford. The whole face of the walk is turned towards the south. The view looks over the Calder Valley rather than towards the Aire which always seems to be Bradford's river. This section also has some common ground with the Calderdale Way. From Oakenshaw the route travels south until it overlooks the M62/M606 junction, having crossed Whitehall Road (again!). Turning west the path goes through Scholes to Bailiff Bridge and then north to Norwood Green. The return route comes back through Wyke to Oakenshaw.

The golf course is Cleckheaton Golf Course and the way over it is fairly obvious but, as always, watch out for the players who have as much right to be there as you. Golf balls can travel remarkably quickly and inflict quite severe injuries, so be careful.

The views over the motorway are quite fascinating and not, I think as horrific as some people find them. But it is strange to go from such a modern setting to one so old fashioned as Scholes. To an outsider, Scholes looks like an isolated village that despite modern housing, time almost seems to have passed by. On the other hand the flavour of Bailiff Bridge is missed because the path only passes through the outskirts. The entrance though is quite unusual as the path goes along the back of some houses before dodging between two of them into Highfield Avenue. After crossing the Whitehall Road for positively the last time the disused Lancashire & Yorkshire railway line from Bradford to Cleckheaton is seen where it crosses the valley on the fine viaduct and shortly the still open Bradford to Halifax line is crossed. After this the path passes the boundary of a cricket field. It then leaves the Calderdale Way to turn sharp left past some stables.

After a (very) short piece of road the route enters Rookes Wood from a field which usually contains some friendly horses. The view from here is surprisingly good and Lightcliffe, Coley and Hipperholme churches can be seen as well as the usual Emley Moor television mast. The wood itself is picturesque and Norwood Green is entered from its small green which contains some comfy seats like Scholes.

The return route travels on the obviously old and now neglected but very beautiful Sowden Lane across Royds Hall Beck. The path which leaves the lane crosses Wyke Tunnel and it is worth pausing to admire another splendid view of the area to the south. Care should be exercised when crossing the A641 because it is a very fast road at this point. Wyke is another of those self-knit communities like Thornton and Idle with which Bradford seems to abound and the route goes through the middle. On occasions while doing this walk my wife and I have paused to do our weekend shopping. This combines business with pleasure and is one reason why we usually take a little haversack with us when we are out walking.

After Wyke the path threads its way through many back streets to emerge alongside some playing fields and a school before coming out on to Wyke Lane near the amazing Allied Colloids Works. At one time it was said that they made three chemicals and you could tell which one a worker was involved with making by the colour of his skin—yellow, brown or red! But I am sure that the tale is apocryphal.

QUEENSBURY
to walk 12
shop
from walk 12
buses
CLAYTON HEIGHTS
Bradford
Scarlet Heights
Highgate Rd.
OLD DOLPHIN
Little Moor
New House Lane
sports ground
golf course
look for stile
Blackshaw Beck Lane
Blackshaw Beck
descend bank
Brighouse Rd. A644
buses
Giles Hill Lane
Brackens Lane
High Cross Lane
Bridge Lane
walk 11
3·5 miles circuit
1·7 m. main route
Cock Hill
look for stile
Odsal A6036 buses
Cock Hill Lane
SHELF
A644 buses
West St.
Shelf Hall Ln.
Bridle stile
Shelf Hall
mill
Bradford Road
Wood Fall Beck
Cross Lane
STONE CHAIR
Ox Heys
Halifax A6036. buses
Brighouse Rd. A644. buses
Calderdale Way
Dean Ho.
North Wood
Coley Road. buses
Coley Beck
walk 10
3·5 miles circuit
1·5 m. main route
The main route follows the Calderdale Way
church
Coley Hall
Coley Hall Lane
Shutts Ln.
to walk 9
from walk 9
NORWOOD GREEN

Walk 10

It is a coincidence that the longest walk on the circuit is followed by the shortest. A walk that goes from Norwood Green through the woods and fields to Shelf and returns through Coley cannot be put on a par with the Pennine Way but it is not without interest.

Norwood Green is an odd village. It seems to sprawl over a very wide area so that it finds it difficult to decide where its centre is. After leaving Norwood Green the path enters North Wood and crosses Wood Fall Beck. Shortly it passes Shelf Hall and the fine Shelf Community Centre before crossing the main Bradford to Halifax road. The return route of this short stroll passes through the centre of Shelf to the district known as Stone Chair. The actual stone chair resides in West Street and was made for passengers waiting for the stage coach.

Coley has virtually no identity at all save for a church, and Coley Hall. The church of St. John dates from the early 16th century when a chapel was built. In 1662 the minister, Oliver Heywood was barred from preaching due to "non-conformity". The chapel was pulled down and the present church built in 1816.

Coley Hall is now inhabited by a Bradford surgeon and is shown to advantage from Coley Hall Lane. It dates from 1649 and with its gateway, archway and mullioned windows looks very well indeed. Back at Norwood Green the houses are of a much younger vintage but there are many fine ones to admire on the way back to the start of the walk.

Walk 11

This is another short walk which could easily be combined with the previous one to make a longer one. It finds a rural route from Shelf to Queensbury which until Littlemoor is reached passes barely a single house. The return via Cock Hill is by an equally rural but more roundabout route.

The path from Shelf to Bridge Lane is unfortunately sometimes very muddy. This is somehat surprising considering its situation almost atop a hill. After a little road work the path takes to the fields again. But as you walk along Brackens Lane a little further a strange triumphal arch can be seen. This was the grand entrance to a drive leading to an old brewery. The path arrives at the Scarlet Heights area of Queensbury. This is the highest point of the walk at fractionally under 1100 feet having climbed all the way from Bailiff Bridge. As befits it there are fine views and Ingleborough can be seen on a clear day. It is only a little way up the road to the John Foster and Sons mill, home of the best Brass Band in the world—Black Dyke.

The return route passes nearby yet another golf course, this time the Queensbury club. The view from Cock Hill is another excellent one and the last which takes in the areas to the south of Bradford including Huddersfield and Holme Moss television aerial—that is the thin one. From here it is a short distance to the starting point in Shelf.

0 1/4 1/2 m.

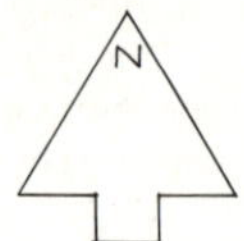

THORNTON

from walk 13
to walk 13
Leventhorpe Hall
Bradford B6145
Thornton Rd. buses
church
grammar school
Denholme
Thornton Hall
modern housing
Clayton beck
Pinch beck
Town End Road
Chat Hill Road
buses
Bradford
Cockin Lane
The Avenue
CLAYTON
Clayton Lane
park
Park Lane & lavs.
Hole Bottom beck
farm
Reva Syke Road
lane
Hole Bottom Farm
Brow Lane
site of old railway station
entrance to old tunnel
Old Gill
Station Road
Baldwin Lane
Clayton Heights
Bradford
shop
buses
Scarlet Heights
Highgate Rd.
Little Moor

QUEENSBURY

from walk 11
to walk 11

walk 12

4·3 miles circuit
1·9 m. main route

Walk 12

Considering the ancient communities of Queensbury, Thornton and Allerton and the historic pathways linking them, the routes of this and the next walk have caused more trouble than the rest of the walks put together. The reason is that the routes fall almost entirely within the old city of Bradford and the definitive maps indicating Rights-of-Way have still not been produced for this area. The route from Scarlet Heights drops down to Queensbury Station and then on footpaths almost directly for Thornton Church. The return route turns towards Bradford and then south to cross Clayton Beck. From Clayton village a footpath is joined which climbs to Baldwin Lane and back to the start.

From Littlemoor the road is crossed and the path passes not only between but underneath two terrace houses! As the hill is descended the main problem area is reached at Old Gill Farm. The large scale maps indicate quite clearly that the path is routed through the garden of the house but a diversion is being planned so walkers should obey any direction signs that may appear after this guide is published.

The old Queensbury Station is a fascinating place as it was a three way junction. It was on the Great Northern line and the lines went (a) to the east to Bradford (b) to the north-west through Thornton to Keighley and (c) through Queensbury Tunnel to Halifax. After passing under the bridge which carried the old Keighley branch railway, Hole Bottom Farm is reached where the owner has carried out extensive repairs and modernisation on the property but throughout has been most careful always to indicate a way for walkers through the works. And it is well worthwhile for the view of the old brick works! Yes, really, the old chimneys (one is pictured on the front cover of this booklet) with their ornate brickwork and ceramics are almost worth making a special journey to see.

Past the dog kennels (loud but not hostile) and across Pinch Beck, Thornton Church is always in view and approached by a pleasant path up the field. The path passes Thornton Hall which is 17th century as is Leaventhorpe Hall on the return route. The church is 19th century and again is prominently situated on the hillside keeping its watch over Bradford.

The return route threads its way on ancient paths through a modern housing estate. These paths which served to link communities now make the lot of the house-wife making for the shops much easier—and the position of the walker more interesting than being threatened by cars the whole time.

The route enters the fields again alongside Leaventhorpe Hall and near Thornton Grammar School. Depending on your like or dislike of school-children, the timing of the walk should be watched carefully for many children walk to school on the path from Clayton.

Unlike Thornton, Clayton is a village which seems to have been overtaken by times. Originally a very old community it seems to have been overwhelmed by the enormous amount of house building that has taken place so that it is now more like a completely new suburb. Thornton, on the other hand still manages in some undefinable way to have maintained its character. Four of the Brontës were born in Thornton. The last hangman lived in Clayton.

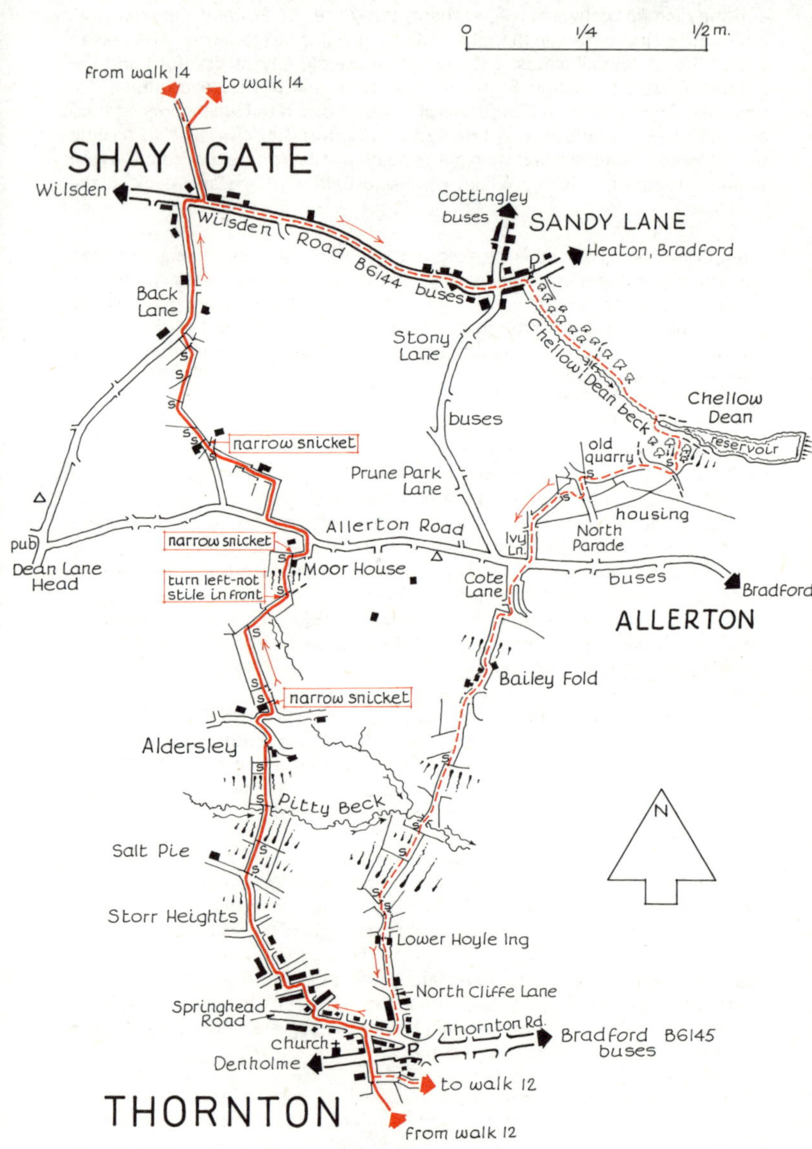

walk 13

5·1 miles circuit
2·2 m. main route

Walk 13

I have never actually been turned off a path on this route despite some of them being almost invisible on the ground. They are rarely used despite being marked on the map and stiles maintained. This is a shame because the route from Thornton to Allerton and on to Wilsden Road is delightful. The return route after the road into Sandy Lane is negotiated, through Chellow Dean to Allerton and on to Thornton is equally splendid.

At Storr Heights a water-shed is crossed. From here, near the charmingly named Salt Pie down the steep hill, Pitty Beck is reached. Pinch Beck, which was crossed on the previous walk joins with Clayton Beck and joins Pitty Beck at Fairweather Green. This is Bradford Beck (i.e. t'mucky beck) which passes underneath the centre of Bradford and joins the Aire in Shipley. Pitty Beck is crossed by a stone slab bridge. Single span versions of these are called clam bridges while multiple span ones are clapper bridges. Both sorts are historic and beautiful to gaze upon.

The steep climb up to Allerton Road passes through the tiny isolated hamlet of Aldersley and follows a very obscure path to Moor House where it goes on a short, high-walled path. On the other side of Allerton Road the path at one point passes between two walls separating a house from part of its garden but the path is clearly marked and well-used. Egypt is not far away! The pub at Dean Lane Head has always been known to me as "Good-Ale-for-Nothing—Tomorrow". The view as Back Lane is approached is fine and again Ingleborough can be seen on a clear day.

The return route has unfortunately to take in a long stretch of main road—about 5/8ths mile to Sandy Lane. The view in all directions in some way compensates for this. The path into Chellow Dean needs little mention for it is well known as a beauty spot. Perhaps it is not as popular as it once was as a place to walk out on a Sunday afternoon because of the gradual encroachment of houses on its periphery but for me it still retains its great charm. Its greatest claim to fame came about 20 years ago when some black swans, a gift from the then Lord Mayor and great Bradford historian, Horace Hird, were imported from Australia, but they are long since gone.

The path threads its way back to Allerton but its emergence on the the main road on North Parade will have more significance for those who travel at a considerably different pace to walkers. This is because it is the home of one of Bradford's very few World Record Holders—Terry Kimber-Smith. Kimber-Smith competes in motor cycle sprint racing where the object is to cover ¼ mile from a standing start as quickly as possible. He competes in the three-wheeler class in a fearsome device powered by a 3½ litre Rover engine which covers the distance in about 12 seconds. The sport can be observed twice a year in the Esholt Sewage Works a short distance from Walk 3, one of the few times when World ranked sportsmen compete in the Bradford area.

From Allerton the path returns to Thornton by way of Bailey Fold. This is another handsome 17th century building with mullioned windows. After crossing Pitty Beck again the path climbs back up to Thornton by which time the walker who has kept properly to the route will have climbed nearly 1000 feet and deserve a cup of tea.

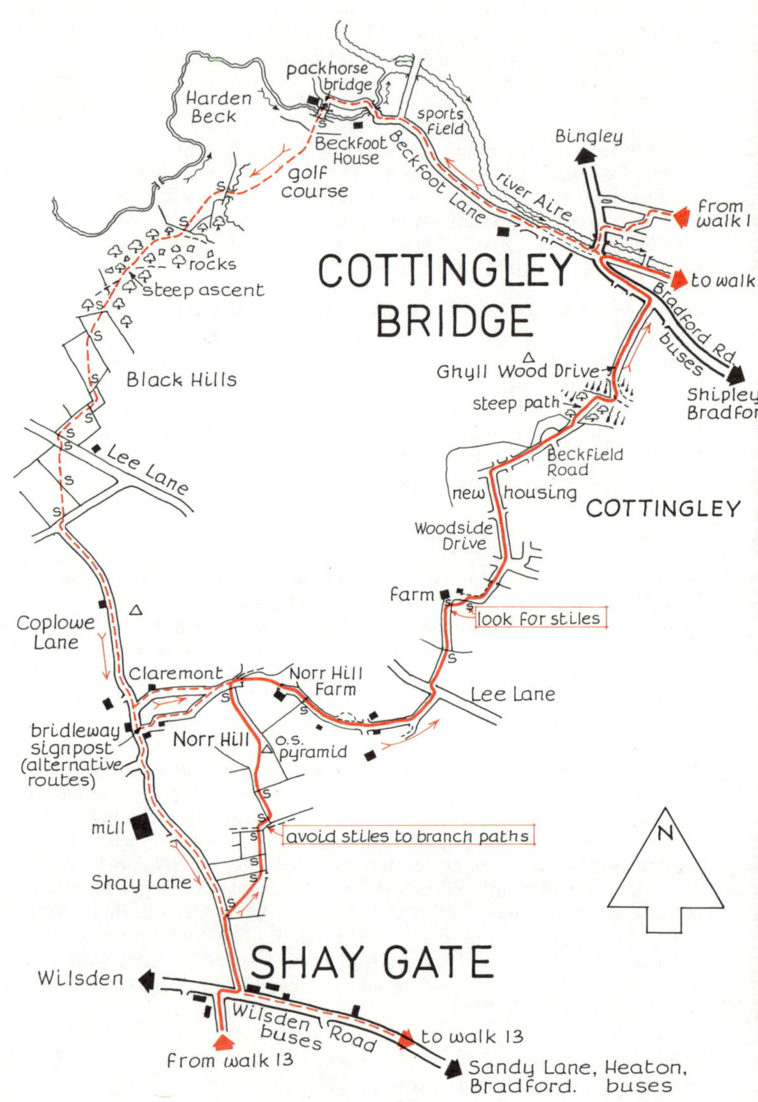

walk 14

4·9 miles circuit
(5·2 via Claremont)
2·3 m. main route

Walk 14

The last walk is a fitting climax. After crossing Norr Hill the route descends through Cottingley to join the start of Walk 1 at Cottingley Bridge. The return route goes along Beckfoot Lane, over the pack horse bridge, across Shipley Golf Course and climbs back up to the shoulder of Norr Hill through the woods adjoining Black Hills Scout Camp.

Norr Hill must not be missed for it provides the best view of the whole walk over Bingley and right up Airedale. Even on a cloudy day the interest of the area round Bingley and St. Ives is worth seeing while on a clear day time should be set by for a pause at this coign of vantage. The descent through Norr Hill Farm features some horses and a noisy but friendly dog. After crossing Lee Lane there are some notices at the farm regarding the path. These should be obeyed but I feel that it is always nicer when folk say ''Please'' on their instructions.

The road through the Cottingley estate cannot be avoided and the road seems very hard if the whole walk has been completed but at least it is downhill. A sweet little path drops down through the woods to the top of Ghyll Wood Drive which emerges on the Bradford to Bingley A650 road at the house with the green roof—surely known to all children who have journeyed regularly along that road. This is also the end of the main route around the city, so anyone wanting to start on a second lap should turn back to Walk 1.

Beckfoot Lane seems surprisingly dangerous for such an innocuous and narrow little lane. As well as being a route used by walkers it also provides access to the Shipley Golf Club and some playing fields further on. Seemingly folk who use these facilities are always in a great hurry because they drive quickly—so beware. After the sports club sanity returns and the charming collection of houses at Beckfoot is reached near the pack horse bridge which crosses Harden Beck. The lantern on the roof of Beckfoot House indicates that the building was once the property of the Knights Hospitallers and therefore was exempted from paying tithes. There is another lantern house on Walk 6 at Tong. The Mill on the other side of the beck has been tastefully converted into flats so possibly the quality of the road (and the amount of traffic it carries) will increase.

The path across the golf course is clearly marked but, as usual it is best to keep a watch for players and flying golf balls. The path enters the woods and climbs steadily on a popular route. The presence of a large number of free-standing boulders provides sure evidence that this part of Yorkshire was once covered by a glacier in times past. On the left, in summer can be seen (and heard) evidence of the Black Hills Scout Camp. This is leased at a peppercorn rent from the Eaton family who own the woods. Whether the fence is present to keep walkers out or campers in is debatable.

When Coplowe Lane is reached it is plain that a short walk along it will take the walker back to the start of the route, not deterred by the fact that the name of the road changes to Shay Lane halfway along. But if sufficient energy remains after the climb, the path alongside Claremont Farm is well worth taking. It goes along one of the superb walled and paved paths which abound in the Wilsden area. Not only this but having gone along the path another visit to the top of Norr Hill cannot be avoided. The result is that the view can be enjoyed for the second time.

PUBLIC TRANSPORT

The convenience of walkers who must use public transport has been an important factor in planning the walks. There is a good Metrobus service from the Interchange to at least one end of each walk. Moreover, there are lateral services near the ends of most walks which make it possible to walk the main route and return to the start by bus, though in some cases two services are involved. Motorists who "park and ride" using these lateral services gain considerably in flexibility.

Indeed, with cheap off-peak fares and frequent services it is hardly worth the bother of getting the car out and finding a parking place, not to mention the cost of petrol, for a motorist who lives in or near the city close to a bus route. Bradford being what it is, a basin with much of the walking round the rim, the relatively high seats of a bus reveal some astonishing vistas.

The **Wayfarer Project** is designed by the West Yorkshire Passenger Transport Executive and the Countryside Commission to encourage people to enjoy the region's magnificent countryside by using the bus and train network at minimal cost. Individual timetable leaflets are available at bus kiosks, inquiry offices and railway stations. There are special off-peak fares on Metrobuses, any distance for 30p (children and pensioners 15p) at early 1982 rates. They are available on Sunday all day; 9.30 to 3 and after 6 on Monday to Friday. Children and pensioners also have Saturdays all day.

For those outside Bradford, the Day Rover ticket at £2 (children and pensioners £1), at early 1982 rates, is valid on any bus or train throughout West Yorkshire.

Metrotrain services between Exchange station, Leeds and the Halifax area (Caldervale line) average three per hour each way, roughly halved on Sundays. The Airedale and Wharfedale lines from Forster Square average three and two per hour respectively, each way, but on Sundays there is no service except in June to August, about five per day.

For further information about the **Wayfarer Project** write to West Yorkshire P.T.E., Metro House, West Parade, Wakefield WF1 1NS.

The Country Code

Enjoy the countryside and respect its life and work.
Guard against all risk of fire.
Fasten all gates.
Keep your dogs under close control.
Keep to public paths across farmland.
Use gates and stiles to cross fences, hedges and walls.
Leave livestock, crops and machinery alone.
Take your litter home.
Help to keep all water clean.
Protect wildlife, plants and trees.
Take special care on country roads.
Make no unnecessary noise.